WILLIAM PENN'S
OWN ACCOUNT
OF THE
LENNI LENAPE
OR
DELAWARE
INDIANS

WILLIAM PENN'S OWN ACCOUNT OF THE LENNI LENAPE OR DELAWARE INDIANS

REVISED EDITION

Edited, and with an introduction
by
Albert Cook Myers

With a foreword by
John E. Pomfret

THE MIDDLE ATLANTIC PRESS
Wallingford, Pennsylvania

This Tercentenary edition owes its existence to the Friendly determination of Dr. Leonore Hollander, the Anna H. and Elizabeth M. Chace Fund Committee of the Philadelphia Yearly Meeting of the Religious Society of Friends, and the Lenape Land Association.

Published by
The Middle Atlantic Press
Box 263
Wallingford, PA 19086

ISBN: 0-912608-13-7
LC: 72-102700

Frontispiece by Fritz Eichenberg
Courtesy of Richmond P. Miller, Philadelphia

CONTENTS

ILLUSTRATIONS

FOREWORD

The Lenni Lenape (Delaware), of whom William Penn wrote in his famous *Account*, were the most important tribe of the Algonquin-speaking Indians of the vast eastern North American woodlands. Their best-known relatives were the Powhatan tribes of Virginia to the south and the Mahicans to the north. The Lenni Lenape or "original people," about 8,000 in number when Penn arrived in 1682, held the territory from lower New York and Long Island to Maryland. Thus they lived on lands from the headwaters of the Delaware River to Delaware Bay and eastward to the ocean, including all of New Jersey, Delaware, and eastern Pennsylvania. Their three main divisions were the Munsee (Wolf totem badge) in the north, the Unami (Turtle) in the center, and Unalachtigo (Turkey) in the south. William Penn dealt with the Unami chiefs along the Delaware.

As Penn mentions, the Lenni Lenape

had met the white man before, principally the Dutch and the Swedes. Unfortunately, irresponsible traders had given them guns and strong drink, both of which they could have done without. The white man's diseases also took a toll among them. The Dutch never got along with the natives. The Indian massacres about Manhattan and west of the Hudson, 1643-1664, were tragic, but the Dutch brought it upon themselves.

The English were determined to establish more amicable relations. Thus East Jersey, West Jersey, and Pennsylvania, the last two colonies founded by Quakers, made it a point of purchasing the Indian title to any lands they wished to settle. Through their early laws they endeavored to prevent traders from cheating the natives and especially to keep strong drink from them. Such laws proved difficult to enforce.

One of Penn's greatest achievements was in his fair dealings with the Indians. He held their loyalty for long years. In 1701, when he was in dire trouble in

England and accused of being a Jacobite, the Lenni Lenape sent a strong testimonial in his behalf addressed to King William and Parliament (Appendix No. 9).

In reading the *Account*, one recognizes immediately that William Penn was an extraordinarily acute observer, interested in all facets of Indian behavior, thinking, and culture. He sat in council with the Indians many times and, in less than a year, he had mastered their language. His comments are of value to anthropologists today. For example, Penn discusses in a sophisticated manner the matriarchal structure of Indian society as well as their religious and moral views. He interprets their mode of living with understanding and sympathy, and adds, somewhat wistfully, "They are not disquieted with Bills of Lading and Exchange, nor perplexed by Chancery-Suits and Exchequer Reckonings." Like many of his contemporaries he thought the Indians descended from the Lost Tribes of Israel who had found their way through Asia to America. Anthropologists now agree that the Indian belonged to the great Mongoloid racial stock whose migration across the Bering Strait began perhaps 50,000 years ago, thus long antedating Israel.

As one of the founders of the Quaker province of West New Jersey, settled in 1677, Penn was aware of the necessity of winning the good-will of the Indians. Indeed, before coming to Pennsylvania, he sent them messages of friendship. Mr. Myers quotes from the *Concessions of West Jersey* (No. 2), prepared by the chief proprietor, Edward Byllynge, with Penn's full knowledge. The pertinent passages state first, that all occupied lands must first be cleared of their Indian title through fair purchase; and secondly, that in case of dispute between the Indian and the settler the trial jury must include six natives. The first was an integral part of Penn's Indian policy, while the latter provision was incorporated in Penn's *Concessions* for Pennsylvania (No. 3). Mr. Myers also includes the chapter of Penn's *Laws of 1682* forbidding the sale of strong liquor to the Indians (No. 5).

Albert Cook Myers (1874-1960), the first modern editor of the *Account*, spent a lifetime researching the American experience of William Penn. In editing this volume, first published in 1937, he included a large number of documents, heretofore unpublished, bearing on Penn's relations with the Indians. In his *Introduction* Mr. Myers provides an excellent statement regarding the provenience of the original document and its first printings in England and on the Continent. There is little that the modern editor would wish to revise. The statement that William Penn was "the foremost Founder of the American Nation" is questionable, but one can forgive Mr. Myers his devotion to the memory of a truly great man. Myers' editing and footnotes, too, are impeccable and add much to our knowledge.

JOHN E. POMFRET

WILLIAM PENN, *by Francis Place*. Thought to be the only authentic likeness of Penn. *Courtesy of the Historical Society of Pennsylvania*

INTRODUCTION

The "Great and Good" William Penn (1644–1718), the Quaker, one of the most illustrious of Englishmen, Founder, Proprietor and Governor of the Province of Pennsylvania, and foremost Founder of the American Nation, is the author of the Account of the Lenni Lenape or Delaware Indians of Pennsylvania which is the main piece of this book. Lord Acton, the eminent English historian, called William Penn "The greatest historic figure of his age," and Tennyson wrote that Penn was "no comet of a season but the fixed light of a dark and graceless age shining on into the present."

Composed in his characteristic, descriptive style, the Account was written by Penn in the Capital of his Province, the infant City of Philadelphia, under date of August (6th Month) 16, 1683, (Old Style, or Julian Calendar), over ten months after his first arrival in America. But recently returned from a general tour of his dominions and particularly having been much occupied for some months in treating with the Indians for their lands, Proprietor Penn was fully informed by personal observation of what he writes. As a first hand authority he is without an equal on the subject for that period.

This description of the Indians is included in a general narrative of his new Province, which he sent over to London in the form of a letter addressed to the Free Society of Traders in Pennsylvania, a land and trading company, incorporated in the latter city by the Proprietor, March 24, 1682, and of which great things were vainly to be expected.

The original manuscript draft of that part[1] of the letter relating to the Indians,

---

[1] In size 7⅝ x 11⅞ inches, containing two large water marks, the one a crown over a fleur-de-lis in a plain shield, above the initials AI, and the other, an ox hunting horn in an ornate shield.

comprised in fourteen folio pages of paper, is wholly in Penn's own handwriting. This draft, which is in possession of The Historical Society of Pennsylvania, in the City of Philadelphia, was filed apparently in the Penn family archives. The letter itself in its final form, with some emendations and slight additions, whether in Penn's hand or that of one of his secretaries is unknown,—for the manuscript letter itself has not been found and doubtless does not exist—was sent over to officers of The Free Society, in England, and published the latter part of the same year in London, with the title, *A Letter from William Penn, Proprietary and Governour of Pennsylvania in America, to the Committee of the Free Society of Traders,* etc.

One of the most important and interesting of Penn's series of Pennsylvania pamphlets, that had its part in the promotion of Pennsylvania colonization, it was issued by the chief Quaker printer and bookseller of that day in London, Andrew Sowle[1] (1628–1695), "at the Crooked-Billet, in Holloway Lane, in Shoreditch". It appeared as a volume, in size 6-⅛ x 10-¼ inches, with a map[2] or plan accompanied by a description of the City of Philadelphia, written by Captain Thomas Holme (1624–1695), Surveyor General of Pennsylvania.

There were four editions[3] of the book issued that same year, 1683, of which three were of ten and the other of four-

---

[1] His apprentice and son-in-law was the noted printer, William Bradford (1663–1752), who coming over to Pennsylvania, in 1685, established his printing press in Philadelphia, where that same year he printed the first book published in America south of New England and north of Mexico.

[2] The original copper plate (in size 18⅜ x 12⅜ inches), from which the map was printed, in 1683, still well preserved, was recently presented by Miss Maria Dickinson Logan, a direct descendant of William Penn's Secretary, James Logan, to The Historical Society of Pennsylvania.

[3] On the title page of the first edition the word Proprietary is misspelled Poprietary.

teen pages. To the latter is appended a long list of property owners in the City, with numbers affixed to the names designating the lots on the plan. In 1684, translations of the book came out in Dutch, German and French. Further bibliographical and like details will be found in Albert Cook Myers, *Narratives of Early Pennsylvania, West New Jersey and Delaware. 1630–1707* (Charles Scribner's Sons, New York, 1912, 8vo., xiv + 476 pages), pages 219–233, and in George Watson Cole, *Church Catalogue, Americana*, iv., 1677–1752 (New York, 1907, 5 volumes, 150 sets), pages 1519–1524.

The present text is from a collation of Penn's original holograph draft with the earliest printed editions of 1683, but the archaic manner of printing certain words in italics has been abandoned for the clearer set-up of Roman type.

ALBERT COOK MYERS

WILLIAM PENN'S
OWN ACCOUNT
OF THE
LENNI LENAPE
OR
DELAWARE
INDIANS

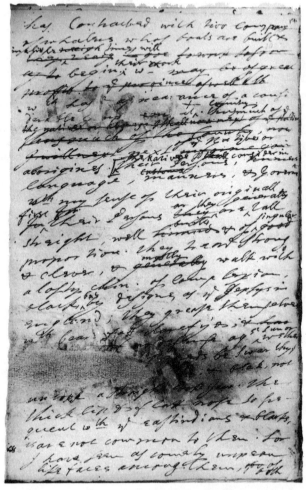

Portion of the first manuscript page of William Penn's
1683 account of the Delaware Indians. Written in his own
hand. *Courtesy of the Historical Society of Pennsylvania*

THE INDIANS

Of the Natives or Aborigines, their Language, Customs and Manners, Diet, Houses or Wigwams, Liberality, easie way of Living, Physick, Burial, Religion, Sacrifices and Cantico, Festivals, Government, and their order in Council upon Treaties for Land, etc., their Justice upon Evil Doers.

THE *Natives* I shall consider in their Persons, Language, Manners, Religion and Government, with my sence of their Original. For their Persons, they are generally tall, streight, well-built, and of singular Proportion; they tread strong and clever, and mostly walk with a lofty Chin: of Complexion, Black, but by design, as the Gypsies in England: They grease themselves with Bears-fat clarified, and using no defence against Sun or Weather, their skins must needs be swarthy; Their Eye is little and black, not unlike a straight-look't Jew. The thick Lip and flat Nose, so frequent with the East-Indians and Blacks, are not common to them; for I have seen as comely European-like faces among them of both, as on your side the Sea; and truly an Italian Complexion hath not much more of the White, and the Noses of several of them have as much of the Roman.

Their Language is lofty, yet narrow, but like the Hebrew; in Signification full, like Short-hand in writing; one word serveth in the place of three, and the rest are supplied by the Understanding of the Hearer: Imperfect in their Tenses, wanting in their Moods, Participles, Adverbs, Conjunctions, Interjections: I have made it my business to understand it, that I might not want an Interpreter on any occasion: And I must say, that I know not

a Language spoken in Europe, that hath
words of more sweetness or greatness, in
Accent and Emphasis, than theirs; for
Instance, *Octorockon*[1], *Rancocas*[2], *Oricton*[3],
Shakamaxon[4], *Poquessin*[5], all of which are
names of Places, and have Grandeur in
them: Of words of Sweetness, *Anna*, is
Mother, *Issimus*, a Brother, *Netap*, Friend,
usque oret, very good; *pone*, Bread, *metse*,
eat, *matta*, no, *hatta*, to have, *payo*, to

---

[1] Octorara Creek, an eastern affluent of Susquehanna River.

[2] Rancocas Creek, an eastern affluent of Delaware River,
Burlington County, New Jersey.

[3] Orectons, now Biles Island, near to the Falls of Delaware
River, and to Penn's country-seat, Pennsbury, in Bucks
County, Pennsylvania.

[4] Shackamaxon, now Kensington, Philadelphia, where Penn
lived for a time, early in 1683, in the house of Thomas Fairman, the surveyor, and where by uncertain tradition, without
record evidence, Penn is alleged to have held treaties with the
Indians.

[5] Poquessing Creek, which flows into Delaware River and
separates Philadelphia from Bucks County.

come; *Sepassen*[1], *Passion*[2], the Names of Places; *Tamany*[3], *Siccane*[4], *Menanse*[5], *Secatareus*[6], are names of Persons. If one ask them for anything they have not, they will answer, *mattá ne hattá*, which to translate is, not I have, instead of I have not.

---

[1] Sepassing Land was the name applied to that part of what is now Bucks County which included Penn's Manor and country-seat of Pennsbury, 25 miles up Delaware River from Philadelphia.

[2] Passyunk was one of the chief locations of the early Lenni Lenape, or Delaware Indians, the Unami group, on the east bank of Schuylkill River, about present Passyunk Avenue, in the City of Philadelphia. There, August 1, 1682, at the house of the noted Indian interpreter, Captain Lasse Cock, of Swedish parentage, a supplementary grant was signed by several Indian chiefs on the back of the deed of July 15, 1682.

[3] Tamany is the form in the original manuscript draft of the *Letter* in Penn's own handwriting, but other variations of the spelling, as appearing in Indian deeds and official documents for the period, 1683–1697, are Tamene, Tamine, Tamina, Tamanee, Tamanen, Tamanend and Taminent. During the above period, to which his authentic history is confined, he was one of the leading chiefs of the Unami group of the Lenni Lenape Indians for the region of Bucks County, Pennsylvania. He with Idquoqueywon, Menangy, and other chiefs, held a preliminary land conference with William Penn, at Perkasie Indian Town, in present Hilltown Township, Bucks County, about May 24 and 25, 1683 (Old Style).

Of their Customs and Manners there is
much to be said; I will begin with Children.
So soon as they are born, they wash them
in Water, and while very young, and in
cold Weather to Chuse, they Plunge them
in the Rivers to harden and embolden

He was a sore trouble to the early settlers of the County and
not at all the amiable figure tradition has made of him.
The Tammany Society of New York City derived its name
from him. He was not living on Penn's second visit to Pennsylvania, 1699–1701.

4 Siccane is the spelling in Penn's hand in the original
draft of the *Letter*, but Secane is the usual spelling. He was
one of the two Unami chiefs granting the region between
Schuylkill River and Chester Creek to Penn, July 14, 1683
(Old Style). In 1685, Penn writes from England that he
sends a cap as a present for "Shikane."

5 Menangy or Menanget, became one of the leading chiefs
of the Unami group of the Lenni Lenape Indians. He with
Idquoqueywon, Tamany, and other chiefs held a preliminary
land conference with William Penn at Perkasie Indian Town,
in present Hilltown Township, Bucks County, about May
24 and 25, 1683 (Old Style).

6 Secatareus as spelled in the original manuscript draft of
the *Letter*, in Penn's hand, was the Indian chief, of Queonemysing Indian Town, in the great bend of Brandywine Creek,
in present Birmingham Township, Delaware County, Pennsylvania, just over the Circular Line of Delaware State. He
and other chiefs sold the land between Christina and Upland
(Chester) Creeks to Penn, December 19, 1683.

them. Having wrapt them in a Clout, they lay them on a straight thin Board, a little more than the length and breadth of the Child, and swadle it fast upon the Board to make it straight; wherefore all Indians have flat Heads; and thus they carry them at their Backs. The Children will go very young, at nine Moneths commonly; they wear only a small Clout round their Waste, till they are big; if Boys, they go a Fishing till ripe for the Woods, which is about Fifteen; then they hunt, and after having given some Proofs of their Manhood, by a good return of Skins, they may Marry, else it is a shame to think of a Wife. The Girls stay with their Mothers, and help to hoe the Ground, plant Corn and carry Burthens; and they do well to use them to that Young, they must do when they are Old; for the Wives are the true Servants of their Husbands: otherwise the Men are very affectionate to them.

When the Young Women are fit for Marriage, they wear something upon their Heads for an Advertisement, but so as their Faces are hardly to be seen, but when they please: The Age they Marry at, if Women, is about thirteen and fourteen; if Men, seventeen and eighteen; they are rarely elder.

Their Houses are Mats, or Bark of Trees[1] set on Poles, in the fashion of an English Barn, but out of the power of the Winds, for they are hardly higher than a Man; they lie on Reeds or Grass. In Travel they lodge in the Woods about a great Fire, with the Mantle of Duffels they wear by day, wrapt about them, and a few Boughs stuck round them.

Their Diet is Maze, or Indian Corn, divers ways prepared: sometimes Roasted in the Ashes, sometimes beaten and Boyled

---

[1] *Mostly chestnut* (crossed off in original draft).

with Water, which they call *Homine;* they also make Cakes, not unpleasant to eat: They have likewise several sorts of Beans and Pease that are good Nourishment; and the Woods and Rivers are their Larder.

If an European comes to see them, or calls for Lodging at their House or *Wigwam* they give him the best place and first cut. If they come to visit us, they salute us with an *Itah* which is as much as to say, Good be to you, and set them down, which is mostly on the Ground, close to their Heels, their Legs upright; maybe they speak not a word more, but observe all Passages: If you give them anything to eat or drink, well, for they will not ask; and be it little or much, if it be with Kindness, they are well pleased, else they go away sullen, but say nothing.

They are great Concealers of their own Resentments, brought to it, I believe, by

the Revenge that hath been practiced
among them; in either of these, they are
not exceded by the Italians. A Tragical
Instance fell out since I came into the
country; A King's Daughter thinking her
self slighted by her Husband, in suffering
another Woman to lie down between them,
rose up, went out, pluck't a Root out of
the Ground, and ate it, upon which she
immediately dyed; and for which, last
Week he made an Offering to her Kindred
for Attonement and liberty of Marriage;
as two others did to kindred of their Wives,
that dyed a natural Death: For till Wid-
dowers have done so, they must not marry
again. Some of the young Women are said
to take undue liberty before Marriage for
a Portion; but when marryed, chaste;
when with Child, they know their Husbands no more, till delivered; and during
their Moneth, they touch no Meat, they
eat, but with a Stick, lest they should

defile it; nor do their Husbands frequent them, till that time be expired.

But in Liberality they excell, nothing is too good for their friend; give them a fine Gun, Coat, or other thing, it may pass twenty hands, before it sticks; light of Heart, strong Affections, but soon spent; the most merry Creatures that live, Feast and Dance almost perpetually; they never have much, nor want much: Wealth circulateth like the Blood, all parts partake; and though none shall want what another hath, yet exact Observers of Property.

Some Kings have sold, others presented me with several[1] parcels of Land; the Pay or Presents I made them, were not hoarded by the particular Owners, but the neighboring Kings and their Clans being present when the Goods were brought out, the Parties chiefly concerned consulted,

---

[1] *4 or 5 parcells* (in the original draft).

what and to whom they should give them?
To every King then, by the hands of a
Person for that work appointed, is a proportion sent, so sorted and folded, and
with that Gravity, that is admirable.
Then that King sub-divideth it in like
manner among his Dependents, they
hardly leaving themselves an Equal share
with one of their Subjects: and be it on
such occasions, at Festivals, or at their
common Meals, the Kings distribute, and
to themselves last. They care for little, because they want but little; and the Reason
is, a little contents them: In this they are
sufficiently revenged on us; if they are
ignorant of our Pleasures, they are also
free from our Pains. They are not disquieted with Bills of Lading and Exchange,
nor perplexed with Chancery-Suits and
Exchequer-Reckonings. We sweat and toil
to live; their pleasure feeds them, I mean,
their Hunting, Fishing and Fowling, and

this Table is spread every where; they eat twice a day, Morning and Evening; their Seats and Table are the Ground. Since the European came into these parts, they are grown great lovers of strong Liquors, Rum especially, and for it exchange the richest of their Skins and Furs: If they are heated with Liquors, they are restless till they have enough to sleep; that is their cry, Some more, and I will go to sleep; but when Drunk, one of the most wretchedst Spectacles in the World,[1] often Burning & Sometimes killing one another, at wch times the Christians are not without danger as well as fear [*Torn*][2].

In sickness impatient to be cured, and for it give anything, especially for their Children, to whom they are extreamly natural; they drink at those times a *Teran* or Decoction of some Roots in spring

---

[1]—[2] In the original draft only.

Water; and if they eat any flesh, it must be of the Female of any Creature; If they dye, they bury them with their Apparel, be they Men or Women, and the nearest of Kin fling in something with them, as a token of their Love: Their Mourning is blacking of their faces, which they continue for a year; They are choice of the Graves of their Dead; for least they should be lost by time, and fall to common use, they pick off the Grass that grows upon them, and heap up the fallen Earth with great care and exactness.

These poor People are under a dark Night in things relating to Religion, to be sure, the Tradition of it; yet they believe in God and Immortality, without the help of Metaphysicks; for they say, There is a great King that made them, who dwells in a glorious Country to the Southward of them, and that the Souls of the good shall go thither, where they shall live again.

Their Worship consists of two parts,
Sacrifice and *Cantico*. Their Sacrifice[1] is
their first Fruits; the first and fattest
Buck they kill, goeth to the fire, where he
is all burnt with a Mournful Ditty of him
that performeth the Ceremony, but with
such marvelous Fervency and Labour of
Body, that he will even sweat to a foam.
The other part is their *Cantico*, performed
by round-Dances, sometimes Words, some-
times Songs, then Shouts, two being in
the middle that begin, and by Singing and
Drumming on a Board direct the Chorus:
Their Postures in the Dance are very
Antick and differing, but all keep measure.
This is done with equal Earnestness and
Labour, but great appearance of Joy.

In the Fall, when the Corn cometh in,
they begin to feast one another; there
have been two great Festivals already[2],

---

[1] *In ye fall* (deleted in the original draft).

[2] *Five* (deleted in the original draft).

to which all come that will: I was at one myself; their Entertainment was a green Seat by a Spring, under some shady Trees, and twenty Bucks, with hot Cakes of new Corn, both Wheat and Beans, which they make up in a square form, in the leaves of the Stem, and bake them in the Ashes: And after that they fell to Dance, But they that go, must carry a small Present in their Money, it may be six Pence, which is made of the Bone of a Fish; the black is with them as Gold, the white, Silver; they call it all *Wampum*.

Their Government is by Kings, which they call *Sachema*, and those by Succession, but always of the Mothers side; for Instance, the Children of him that is now King, will not succeed, but his Brother by the Mother, or the Children of his Sister, whose Sons (and after them the Children of her Daughters) will reign; for no Woman inherits; the Reason they render for this way of Descent, is, that their Issue may not be spurious.

Every King hath his Council, and that consists of all the Old and Wise men of his Nation, which perhaps is two hundred People: nothing of Moment is undertaken, be it War, Peace, Selling of Land or Traffick, without advising with them; and which is more, with the Young Men too. 'Tis admirable to consider, how Powerful the Kings are, and yet how they move by the Breath of their People.

I have had occasion to be in Council with them upon Treaties for Land, and to adjust the terms of Trade; their Order is thus: The King sits in the middle of an half Moon, and hath his Council, the Old and Wise on each hand; behind them, or at a little distance, sit the younger Fry, in the same figure. Having consulted and resolved their business, the King ordered one of them to speak to me; he stood up, came to me, and in the Name of his King saluted me, then took me by the hand, and told me, That he was ordered by his King to speak to me, and that now it was not he, but the King that spoke, because what he should say, was the King's mind. He first pray'd me, To excuse them that they had not complyed with me the last time; he feared, there might be some fault in the Interpreter, being neither Indian nor English; besides, it was the Indian Custom to deliberate, and take up much time in Council, before they resolve; and that if the Young People and Owners of the Land had been as ready as he, I had not met with so much delay. Having thus introduced his matter, he fell to the Bounds of the Land they had agreed to dispose of, and the Price, (which now is little and dear, that which would have bought twenty Miles, not buying now two.) During the time that this Person spoke, not a man of them was observed to whisper or smile; the Old, Grave, the Young, Reverend in their Deportment; they do speak little, but fervently, and with Elegancy: I have never seen more natural Sagacity, considering them without the help, (I was agoing to say, the spoil) of Tradition; and he will deserve the Name of Wise, that Outwits them in any Treaty about a thing they understand.

[1]When the Purchase was agreed, great Promises past between us of Kindness and good Neighbourhood, and that the Indians and English must live in Love, as long as the Sun gave light. Which done, another made a Speech to the Indians, in the Name of all the *Sachamakers* or Kings, first to tell them what was done; next, to charge and command them, To Love the Christians, and particularly live in Peace

---

[1]—[2] This paragraph not in the original draft.

with me, and the People under my Government: That many Governors had been in the River, but that no Gouvernour had come himself to live and stay here before; and having now such a one that had treated them well, they should never do him or his any wrong. At every sentence of which they shouted, and said, Amen, in their way.[2]

The Justice they have is Pecuniary: In case of any Wrong or evil Fact, be it Murther it self, they Attone by Feasts and Presents of their *Wampum*, which is proportioned to the quality of the Offence or Person injured, or of the Sex they are of: for in case they kill a Woman, they pay double, and the Reason they render, is, That she breedeth Children, which men cannot do. 'Tis rare that they fall out, if Sober; and if Drunk, they forgive it, saying, It was the Drink, and not the Man, that abused them.

We have agreed, that in all Differences between us, Six of each side shall end the matter: Don't abuse them, but let them have Justice, and you win them: The worst is, that they are the worse for the Christians, who have propagated their Vices, and yielded them Tradition for ill, and not for good things. But as low an Ebb as they are at, and as glorious as their Condition looks, the Christians have not out-liv'd their sight with all their Pretensions to an higher Manifestation: What good then might not a good People graft, where there is so distinct a Knowledge left between Good and Evil? I beseech God to incline the Hearts of all that come into these parts, to out-live the Knowledge of the Natives, by a fixt Obedience to their greater Knowledge of the Will of God; for it were miserable indeed for us to fall under the just censure of the poor Indian Conscience, while we

make profession of things so far trans-
cending.

[1]For their Original, I am ready to believe them of the Jewish Race, I mean, of
the stock of the Ten Tribes, and that for
the following Reasons; first, They were to
go to a Land not planted or known, which
to be sure Asia and Africa were, if not
Europe; and he that intended that
extraordinary Judgment upon them,
might make the Passage not uneasie to
them, as it is not impossible in it self, from
the Easter-most parts of Asia, to the
Wester-most of America. In the next
place, I find them of like Countenance and
their Children of so lively Resemblance,
that a man would think himself in Dukes-
place[3] or Berry-street[3] in London, when
he seeth them. But this is not all, they

---

[1]—[2] Not in the original draft.

[3] Then as now these streets were in the centre of a Jewish
quarter.

agree in Rites, they reckon by Moons: they offer their first Fruits, they have a kind of Feast of Tabernacles; they are said to lay their Altar upon twelve Stones; their Mourning a year, Customs of Women, with many things that do not now occur.

So much for the Natives.[2]

———

[1]"For the People [the Indians]; they are Savage to us, in their Persons, & furniture; all y^t is rude; but they have great shape, Strength, agility; and in Councel (for they (tho in a kind of Community, among them selves) observe property & Governm^t.) grave, Speak Seldom, inter spaces of silence, Short, Elegant, fervent, the old sitt in a half moon upon ye Ground, the middle aged in a like figure at a little distance behind them, & the young Fry in the same manner behind them. None speak but the Aged, they haveing Consulted the rest before; thus in selling me their land they order'd themselves; I must say, y^t obscurity Consider'd, wanting tradition, Example & instruction, they are an

———

[1] From William Penn's holograph letter, in an English collection, dated Philadelphia, 5th month (July) 28, 1683, addressed to the friend of his youth, in France, Robert Spencer (1640–1702), 2nd Earl of Sunderland, in England.

Extreordinary people; had not the Dutch, Sweeds and English learn'd them drunkenness (in wch. condition, they kill or burn one another) they had been very tractable, but Rum is so dear to them, y^t for 6 penny worth of Rum, one may buy y^t Furr from them, y^t five Shillings, in any other Commodity shall not purchass. yet many of the old men, & some of ye young people will not touch wth such Spirits; & Because in thos fitts they mischeif both themselves & our folks too, I have forbid to sell them any."

———

[1]"The Natives are proper & shapely, very swift their language lofty. The[y] speak little but fervently & with Elegancy I have never seen more naturall sagacity considering them wth out ye I was going to say ye spoyle of Tradition. The worst is that they are ye wors for ye Christians who have propagated their views and yeilded them tradition for ye wors & not for ye better things, they beleive a Diety & Immortality without ye help of Metaphisicks & some of them admirably sober though ye Dutch & Sweed[s] and English have by Brandy and Rum almost Debaucht y^m all and when Drunk ye most wretched of Spectacles often burning & some-

---

[1] From a contemporary copy of a letter, in the hand of a secretary, from William Penn, dated Philadelphia, 5th Month (July) 30, 1683, to Henry Savell, in England. (H. S. P.)

times murdering one another at which times y^e
Christians are not without danger as well as fear.
Tho' for gain they will runn ye hazard both of
y^t and ye Law they make their worshipp to
Consist of two parts Sacrifices wch they offer of
their first fruits with marvelous fervency and
Labour of body sweating as if in a Bath The
other is their Canticoes as they Call them w^{ch}
is performed by round Dances sometimes words
then songs then shouts two being in ye midle y^t
begin & direct ye chorno this they performe with
equall fervency but great appearances of Joy.

In this I admire them nobody shall want w^t
another has yett they propriety, but freely
comunicable they want or Care for Little No
Bills of Exchange nor Bills of Lading no Chancery siuts nor Exchequer Acc^t have they to per-
plex themselfs with they are soon satisfyed and
their pleasure feeds them I mean hunting & fishing I have made two purchases And have had
two p^{r}sents of land from them."

———

[1]"I find them [the Indians] a people rude, to
Europeans, in dress, gesture, and food; but of a
deep natural sagacity, Say little, but what they
speak is fervent and elegant; if they please, close

———

[1] From a letter of William Penn, dated Philadelphia, 6th
Month (August) 5, 1683, to his scientific friend, Robert Boyle
(1627–1691), son of Richard Boyle, 1st Earl of Cork.—*Works
of Robert Boyle*, V. (London, 1744), 646.

to the point, and can be as evasive. In treaties, about land, or traffick, I find them deliberate in council, and as designing, as I have ever observed among the politest of our Europeans. I have bought two large tracts, and had two presented me, which cost me alike. However, in this they are happy, and even with us, they care and want for little; and if they have not had their passions raised to the same degree after the luxury of Europe, by like enjoyments, neither have they the anxieties that follow those pleasures. They trouble not themselves about bills of lading, or exchange; nor are they molested with chancery suits and exchequer accounts. Their rest is not disturbed for maintenance; they live by their pleasures, fowling and fishing; the sons of providence; better without tradition, unless that they have got had been better; for the Dutch, English, and Swedes have taught them drunkenness. Thus they are the worse for those they should have been the better for; and this they are not so dark as not to see and say. So that the low dispensation of the poor Indian out shines the lives of those Christians, that pretend an higher."

APPENDIX

I

WILLIAM PENN'S DESCRIPTION OF THE SWEAT BATH OF INDIAN CHIEF TENOUGHAN, IN PENNSYLVANIA, THE WINTER OF 1683-4, ABOUT 11TH MONTH (JANUARY) (OLD STYLE).

The cold bath of Indian Chief Tenoughan, here described by Penn, occurred in the Proprietor's journey "upon a Discovery of the back part of the Country," in the winter of 1683-4, about January, at the time of the notable "great Frost," even in London, England, the River Thames being frozen over so that booths were erected upon the ice. It was in this winter season that Penn was living at Shackamaxon, now Kensington, Philadelphia, in the house, on Delaware River bank, of the Deputy Surveyor of the Province, Thomas Fairman; the latter enters in his accounts against Penn the item, "To the Leaving my House in the Winter Season for the Proprietors use." Fairman also follows with the entry, "To a Journey with the Proprietor & taking the Courses of Scholkill [River] above the Town [of Philadelphia]."

In an unpublished holograph letter, in an English collection, dated Philadelphia, 2nd Month, (April) 3, 1684, Penn writes, "I can say of my own Knowledge, yᵗ for 50 miles up Skulkill [River] falls, generally, one acre is worth two on delaware [River], & often more." Measuring up the courses of Schuylkill River from the Falls of the River reaches a point at the present Town of Monocacy, near the mouth of Monocacy Creek, an eastern affluent of Schuylkill River, in what is now Amity Township, Berks County. To the eastward, a striking landmark, rises the picturesque, wooded cone of Monocacy Hill.

From these facts, together with a long and intensive study

of Penn's Pennsylvania itinerary, which I have compiled, I am of the opinion that Monocacy was Penn's fartherest north in his Province during his two American sojourns. Near by to the eastward, on the main State Highway, in commemoration of this conclusion, a great stone and bronze marker was erected by The Pennsylvania State Historical Commission and The Berks County Historical Society, in 1926.

In an elaborate investigation of all known early Pennsylvania Indian deeds and of the chiefs concerned in the sale of their lands to Penn, Chief Tenoughan does not appear as a grantor of land in any of the deeds, but simply as one of the seven witnesses—spelled "Tenoughant"—of the "Great men of the Indians," to the deed of 5th Month (July) 20, 1685, by which Secane and other chiefs sold to Penn the land between Chester Creek and Pennypack Creek.

Surveyor General Thomas Holme's letter, dated 5th Month (July) 7, 1688, concerning the running of a survey line, addressed to the latter chiefs, includes "Tenoughan" and is endorsed:

"Thomas Holme
To the Sculkill Indians."

As a chief of the Schuylkill River hinterland Tenoughan, it would seem, had not yet granted Penn his remote region.

A consideration of the topography of the Town of Monocacy and the neighboring Schuylkill River region not only points to the site of the Town as an excellent location for an Indian town but the numerous Indian artifacts, including those of the village type, found there show definitely that an aboriginal town once stood at present Monocacy.

So that when William Penn reached his fartherest north in Pennsylvania, at Monocacy, it is possible that it was in this winter of 1683–4, that he found there an Indian town, and that it was the village of Chief Tenoughan, whose wigwam Penn saw standing 40 paces (or about 100 feet) from the River.

Penn's Description

"For being upon a Discovery of the back part of the Country, I called upon an Indian of Note, whose Name was Tenoughan, the Captain General of the Clan of Indians of those Parts. I found him ill of a Fever, his Head and Limbs much affected with Pain, and at the same time his Wife preparing a Bagnio for him: The Bagnio resembled a large Oven, into which he crept, by a Door on the one side, while she put several red hot Stones in a small Door on the other side thereof, and then fastned the Doors as closely from the Air as she could. Now while he was Sweating in this Bagnio, his Wife (for they disdain no Service) was, with an Ax, cutting her Husband a passage into the River, (being the Winter of 83 the great Frost, and the Ice very thick) in order to the Immersing himself, after he should come out of his Bath. In less than half an Hour, he was in so great a Sweat, that when he came out he was as wet, as if he had come out of a River, and the Reak or Steam of his Body so thick, that it was hard to discern any bodies Face that stood near him. In this condition, stark naked (his Breech-Clout only excepted) he ran to the River, which was about twenty Paces, and duck'd himself twice or thrice therein, and so return'd (passing only through his Bagnio to mitigate the immediate stroak of the Cold) to his own House, perhaps 20 Paces further, and wrapping himself in his woolen Mantle, lay down as his length near a long (but gentle) Fire in the midst of his Wigwam, or House, turning himself several times, till he was dry, and then he rose, and fell to getting us our Dinner, seeming to be as easie, and well in Health, as at any other time."

This same account, with some elaboration, is thus given by one of William Penn's English contemporaries, John Oldmixon (1673–1742), in his "British Empire of America" (London, 1708), pages 161–162:

"They [the Indians] have a great Opinion of Cold Baths and Sweatings: An Instance of which we shall report, it being very extraordinary, and the Truth of it is not to be questioned; for the Gentleman who told it to us, was the very Person that saw it. Mr. Pen. in the Year 1683, travelling into the Back Countries, to make Discoveries, came to a Wigwam, where the Captain General of that Nation liv'd; for they have such an Officer, besides their Sachem or King, who commands the Army, and leads them to Battle: The Captain General happen'd to be at that time ill of a Fever, and was about to try their usual Remedy to cure himself. His Wife to that end had prepar'd a little Bagnio upon the Ground, without Doors, into which he crept. This Bagnio was like an Oven; and his Wife, to heat it, put several great hot Stones on each side of it, which gave the Man an extream Sweat, while he sat or lay along in this Oven or Bagnio. She made a Hole through the Ice of the River, it being frosty Weather, and the Bagnio on the River's Bank. This Hole or Passage she dug with an Axe, the Ice being very thick. When the Passage was prepar'd, the Man came out of his Oven, the Drops of Sweat running down his Face and Body, leapt into the River, and duckt himself twice. He then crept through his Oven, and so went to his Wigwam, where laying himself down by a Fire, he gradually cool'd himself, and was afterwards as well as ever.

Thus far we have told this Story, to shew what Opinion the Indians have of Sweating and Cold Baths: The remaining part of it is to give the Reader an Idea of their Manners and Understanding; and being assur'd by Mr. Pen himself, that the following Relation is true, we recommend it as such to the World, for we cannot have better Authority.

While the Captain General was in the Bagnio, he first sang all the Acts of the Nation he was of, to divert him from the Troublesomeness of the Heat; then those of his Ancestors, who were Nobles and Generals in the Country; and last of all, his own. After which he fell into this Rhapsody: *What is the Matter with us Indians, that we are thus sick in our own*

Air, and these Strangers well? 'Tis as if they were sent hither to inherit our Lands in our steeds; but the Reason is plain, they love the great God, and we do not. A Reflection very surprizing in a Barbarian; but Mr. Pen heard it, and attested it to be Matter of Fact to the Historian."

THE HEART-HAND OF GREETING, *by William Sauts Netamuxwe Bock, 1980.* The Lenape leaders assembled inside the Big House at Perkasie to greet William Penn. Idquoqueywon has risen to extend his heart-hand (the left hand). *Courtesy of the Lenape Land Association.*

2

INDIAN RELATIONS, FROM WILLIAM PENN'S CON-
CESSIONS AND AGREEMENTS OF WEST NEW
JERSEY, MARCH (1ST MONTH, OLD STYLE, OR
JULIAN CALENDAR) 3, 1675–6.

Chapter 25[1]

That there may be a good vnderstanding and friendly
correspondence between the proprietors freeholders and
inhabitants of the said province and the Indian Natives thereof

It is concluded and agreed that if any of the Indian natives
within the said province shall or may doe any wrong or injury
to any of the Proprietors ffreeholders or inhabitants in person
estate or otherwayes howsoever vpon notice thereof or Complaint made to the commissioners or any two of them they
are to give notice to the Sachim or other chiefe person or
persons that hath authority over the said Indian native or
natives that Justice may be done and satisfaction made to
the Person or persons offended according to Law and Equitie
and the nature and quallitie of the offence and injury done or
comitted. And also in case any of the Proprietors ffreeholders
or Inhabitants shall any wise wrong or injure any of the
Indian natives there in person estate or otherwise the Comissioners are to take care vpon complaint to them made or
any one of them either by the indian natives or others that
Justice be done to the Indian Natives and plenary satisfaction
made them according to the nature and quallite of the offence
and Injury And that in all tryalls wherein any of the said
Indian Natives are concerned the tryall to be by six of the
neighbourhood and six of the said Indian Natives to be
indifferently and impartially Chosen by order of the Comis-

[1] Pages 62–65.

sioners and that the Comissioners use their endeavour to persuade the Natives to the like way of tryall when any of the Natives doe any waies wrong or injure the said proprietors ffreeholders or inhabitants that they choose six of the Natives and six of the ffreeholders or Inhabitants to Judge of the wrong and injury done and to proportion satisfaction accordingly.

Chapter 26[1]

It is agreed when any land is to be taken up for settlement of townes or otherwayes before it be Surveyed the Comissioners or the major part of them are to appoint some persons to goe to the chiefe of the natives concerned in that land soe intended to be taken up to acquaint the Natives of their Intention and to give the Natives what present they shall agree upon for their good will or consent and take a grant of the same in writeing under their hands and seales or some other publick way used in those parts of the world which grant is to be Registered in the publick register allowing alsoe Natives (if they please) a coppie thereof and that noe Person or persons take up any land but by order from the Comissioners for the time being."

---

[1] Pages 65–67, the original calf-bound vellum volume, in size 9¾ x 12⅞ x 1¼ inches, in possession of the Council of Proprietors of the West Division of New Jersey, Surveyor General's Office, Burlington, New Jersey.

3

INDIAN SECTIONS IN CERTAIN CONDITIONS OR
CONCESSIONS AGREED UPON BETWEEN WILLIAM
PENN AND HIS PENNSYLVANIA LAND PURCHASERS,
5TH MONTH (JULY) 11, 1681 (OLD STYLE).[1]

13.ly That noe man shall by any wayes or meanes in word
or Deed, affront or wrong any Indian, but he shall Incurr
the Same Pennalty of the Law as if he had Comitted it
against his ffellow Planter, & if any Indian shall abuse in
word or deed any planter of this province, that he shall not
be his owne Judge upon the Indian, but he shall make his
Complt. to the Governcr. of the Province or his Lieutenant
or Deputy, or some Inferiour Magistrate neare him, who
shall to the uttmost of his power, Take Care with the King
of the sd. Indian; that all reasonable Sattisfaccon be made to
the said Injured Planter.

14ly. That all differences between the planters and the
Natives shall also be ended by Twelve men, that is by six
Planters and Six Natives, that so we may Live friendly To-
gether, and as much as in us Lyeth, Prevent all occasions of
Heart Burnings and mischeifs.

15ly. That the Indians shall have Liberty to doe all things
Relateing to ye Improvemt. of ye ground & providing Sus-
tenance for yr. ffamilyes, that any of ye planters shall enjoy.

---

[1] From a contemporary copy in a private collection.

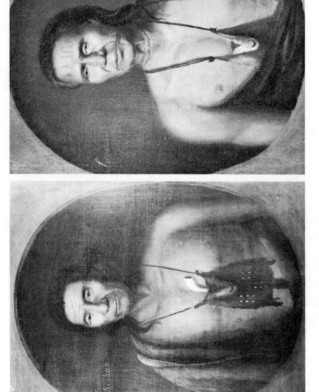

TISHCOHAN (left) and LAPOWINSA, *by Gustavus Hesselius, 1735.* Delaware chiefs who signed the treaty of 1737, known as the "Walking Purchase." Painted from life. *Courtesy of the Historical Society of Pennsylvania*

4

FROM WILLIAM PENN'S INSTRUCTIONS TO HIS
PENNSYLVANIA COMMISSIONERS, DATED 7TH
MONTH (SEPTEMBER) 30, 1681 (OLD STYLE).[1]

9[thly] Be tender of offending the Indians, and hearken by
honest Spyes, if you can hear y[t] any body inveighs y[e] Indians
not to sell, or to stand off, and raise the vallue upon you.
You cannot want those y[t] will informe you, but to sofften
them to mee and the people, lett them know y[t] you are come
to sitt downe Lovingly among them. Let my Letter and
Conditions w[th]: my Purchasers about just dealing with them
be read in their Tongue, that they may see, wee have their
good in our eye, equall w[th]: our owne Interest, and after
reading my Letter, and y[e.] said Conditions, then present
their Kings w[th]: what I send them, and make a Friendshipp
and League wth them according to those Conditions, w[ch]
carefully observe, and get them to comply wth you; be Grave
they love not to be smiled on.

10[thly] From time to time in my Name and for my use buy
Land of them, where any justly pretend, for they will sell one
anothers, if you be not Carefull, that so such as buy and
come after these Adventurers may have Land ready but by
no means sell any Land till I come

DATED LONDON 8TH MONTH (OCTOBER) 28, 1681
(OLD STYLE).[2]

Memorãnd. of Additionall Instructions to Wm Markham
& Wm Crispin & J[no.] Bezer

---

[1] D. S. of William Penn, in H.S.P.; also same Instructions,
dated 8th Month (October) 14, 1681, in the hand of Samuel
Carpenter, in the Albert Cook Myers Collection.

[2] Now first printed, from the original contemporary copy,
in the hand of Samuel Carpenter (1647–1714), in the Albert
Cook Myers Collection.

ffirst, To Act all in my Name as Proprietary & Gov^{r}n^r

Secondly To buy Land of the true Owners w$^{ch.}$ I think is the Susquehanna People

Thirdly To treat Speedily w$^{th.}$ the Indians for Land before they are ffurnisht by Others w$^{th.}$ things that Please y^m take advice in this.

* * *   28.8:$\frac{0}{mo}$ 1681 at London

Witnesses: W^m. Penn

George ffox, Richard Davies, Christ^o. Taylor

                                   Tho: Rudyard

5

WILLIAM PENN'S GREAT LAW, PASSED BY HIS
FIRST LEGISLATIVE ASSEMBLY OF PENNSYLVANIA,
AT UPLAND (CHESTER), 10TH MONTH (DECEMBER)
5, 1682 (OLD STYLE), FORBIDDING THE SALE OF
RUM TO THE INDIANS.[1]

Chapter "18. Whereas divers Persons as English Dutch
Sweedes &c: have been wont to sell to yᵉ Indians Rhum &
brandy and Such like distill'd Spiritts though they know yᵉ
said Indians are not able to govern themselves in yᵉ use
thereof but doe comonly drink of it to such excess as makes
them sometimes to destroy one another & greiviously anoy
and disquiet yᵉ People of this Province & Peradventure those
of Neighbouring Governmᵗˢ. whereby they make yᵉ Poor
Natives worse and not better for their Coming among them
which is an heinious offence to God & is a Reproach to yᵉ
blessed name of Christ and his holy Religion It is therefore
enacted by yᵉ Authority aforesᵈ that no person within this
Province doe from hence forth presume to Sell or exchange
any Rhum or brandy or any Strong Liquors at any time to
any Indian within this Province & if any one shall offend
therein yᵉ person convicted Shall for every Such offence pay
five pounds"

------

[1] From the original MS. in the Division of Public Records,
Harrisburg, Pennsylvania.

6

WILLIAM PENN'S LETTER TO THE PENNSYLVANIA INDIANS, DATED LONDON, 8TH MONTH, (OCTOBER) 18, 1681 (OLD STYLE).[1]

Lond : 18th—8 ^{mo}—81

My Freinds—

There is one great God and Power that hath made ye world and all things therein, to whom you and I and all People owe their being and well being, and to whom you and I must one Day give an account, for all that we do in this world: this great God hath written his law in our hearts, by which we are taught and commanded to love and help and do good to one another and not to do harme and mischeif one unto one an other.

Now this great God hath been pleased to make me concerned in your parts of the world, and the king of the Countrey where I live, hath given unto me a great Province therein, but I desire to enjoy it with your Love and Consent, that we may always live together as Neighbours and freinds, else what would the great God say to us, who hath made us not to devoure and destroy one an other but live soberly and kindly together in the world. Now I would have well to observe, that I am very sensible of the unkindness and Injustice that hath been too much exersised toward you by the People of thes Parts off the world, who have sought themselves, and to make great Advantages by you, rather then be examples of justice & goodness unto you, which I hear hath been a matter of Trouble to you, and caused great Grudgings and Animosities, sometimes to the shedding of blood, which hath made the great God Angry. but I am not such a man, as is

---

[1] From the original, of two pages, in size 8 x 12¼ inches, in the hand of a secretary but signed by Penn himself. (H.S.P.)

well known in my own Country: I have great love and regard towards you, and I desire to winn and gain your Love and freindship by a kind, just and peaceable life; and the People I send are of the same mind, & shall in all things behave themselves accordingly; and if in any thing any shall offend you or your People, you shall have a full and Speedy Satisfaction for the same, by an equal number of honest men on both sides that by no means you may have just occasion of being offended against them;

I shall shortly come to you myselfe. At what time we may more largely and freely confer & discourse of these matters; in the mean time I have sent my Commissioners to treat wth you about land & a fir[m] league of peace, lett me desire you to be kind to them & ye People, and receive the Presents and Tokens which I have sent to you, as a Testimony of my Good will to you, and my resolution to live Justly pea[ce]ably and freindly with you,

I am your freind
Wm Penn

Addressed in William Penn's hand:

For the Kings
of the Indians
in Pennsylvania.

7

WILLIAM PENN'S LETTER TO THE INDIANS OF PENNSYLVANIA, DATED ENGLAND, 2ND MONTH (APRIL) 21, 1682 (OLD STYLE).

From the original vellum, 12⅝ x 9⅞ inches, in possession of The Delaware Historical Society, Wilmington, Delaware. It is in the hand of his Saxon secretary, Mark Swanner (1639—1713), a London Quaker, save for the last line, place, date, and subscription, which are in Penn's own hand.

[1] The Great God who is the power and wisdom that made you and me, Incline your hearts to Righteousness, Love and peace. This I send to Assure you of my Love, and to desire your Love to my ffriends, and when the Great God brings me among you I intend to order all things in such manner, that we may all live in Love and peace one with another, which I hope the Great God will Incline both me and you to do. I seek nothing but the hono[r]. of his name, and that we who are his Workmanship, may do that which is well pleasing to him. The man which delivers this unto you, is my Special ffriend, Sober wise and Loving, you may believe him. I have already taken Care that none of my people wrong you, by good Laws I have provided for that purpose, nor will I ever allow any of my people to sell Rumme to make your people Drunk. If anything should be out of order, expect when I come, it shall be mended, and I will bring you some-things of our Country, that are useful and pleasing to you. [2]So I rest In y[e] Love of our god yt made us I am

Your Loveing Friend

England 21: 2[mo]: 1682   Wm Penn[3]

---

[1]—[2] is in the hand of Penn's Saxson secretary, Mark Swanner, a Quaker, long resident in England.

[3]—[3] is in the hand of Penn himself.

[1] I read this to the Indians
   by an Interpreter the
      6 mo 1682 Tho : Holme[2]

---

[1]—[2] is in the hand of Captain Thomas Holme (1624–1695), Quaker, first Surveyor General of Pennsylvania, a native of England and sometime Cromwellian soldier in Ireland. He had arrived in Pennsylvania in the ship *Amity* in the early summer of 1682.

8

WILLIAM PENN'S LETTER TO A LEADING PENN-
SYLVANIA INDIAN CHIEF, WHOM HE ADDRESSES
AS THE EMPEROR OF CANADA, DATED LON-
DON, 4TH MONTH (JUNE) 21, 1682 (OLD STYLE).

*From the original manuscript, in size 29 x 22½ inches, in the
Division of Public Archives, State Library, Harrisburg, Pennsylvania. It is beautifully engrossed by a contemporary
scrivener, but signed in their own handwriting both by Penn
himself and his Saxson secretary, Philip Theodore Lehmann
(d. 1687). The latter, a Quaker, sometime of Bristol, England,
came over with Penn to Pennsylvania, in 1682, and died there.*

To the Emperor of Canada.

The Great God that made thee and me and all the World
Incline our hearts to love peace and Justice that we may
live friendly together as becomes the workmanship of the
great God. The King of England who is a Great Prince hath
for divers Reasons Granted to me a large Country in America
which however I am willing to Injoy upon friendly termes
with thee. And this I will say that the people who comes
with me are a just plain and honest people that neither make
war upon others nor fear war from others because they will
be just. I have sett up a Society of Traders in my Province
to traffick with thee and thy people for your Comodities that
you may be furnished with that which is good at reasonable
rates And that Society hath ordered their President [Dr.
Nicholas More (c.1638–1687)] to treat with thee about a
future Trade and have joined with me to send this Messenger
to thee with certain Presents from us to testify our Willingness
to have a fair Correspondence with thee: I hope thou wilt
kindly Receive him and Comply with his desires on our behalf

both with Respect to Land and Trade. The Great God be
with thee. Amen.

Wm Penn

Philip Theodore Lehnmann, Secret^y

London the 21$^{st.}$ day of
the ffourth Month called
June 1682.

9

LETTER OF PENNSYLVANIA INDIANS TO THE KING
OF ENGLAND COMMENDING THEIR FRIEND WIL-
LIAM PENN, 1701.

*In the hand of James Logan, with the marks of the chiefs
themselves. Endorsed in Penn's hand: "The Indian Kings
Address to the King and Parliam^t." (H.S.P.). The transcript:*

We the Kings and Sachems of the Ancient Nations of the
Sasquehannah and Shavanah Indians, understanding that
our Loving and good ffriend and Brother William Penn is to
our great Grief and the trouble of all the Indians of these
parts obliged to goe back for England to speak with the great
King and his Sachems about his Governm^t can doe no less
than acknowledge that he has been not only alwayes just
but very kind to us as well as our ancient Kings and Sachems
deceased, & careful to keep a good Correspondence with us,
not suffering us to receive any Wrong from any of the People
under his Governm^t, Giving us as is well known, his House
for our Home at all times and freely entertaining us at his
own Cost and often filling us with many presents of necessary
Goods for our Cloathing, & other Accommodations, besides
what he has paid us for our Lands, which no Govern^r ever
did before him, and we hope and desire that the great King
of ye English will be good and kind to him and his Children,
and grant that they may alwayes Govern these parts, and
then we shall have Confidence, That we and our Children and
People will be well used and be encouraged to continue to live
among the Christians according to the Agreem^t. that he and
We have solemnly made for us and our Posterity as long as
the Sun and the Moon shall endure, One head One Mouth,
and one Heart. We could say much more of his good Council
and Instructions, which he has often given us and our People

to live a Sober & Virtuous Life as the best Way to please the great God and be happy here and for ever But lett this Suffice to the great King and his wise Sachems in love to our good ffriend and Brother William Penn.

Deliverd to the Governer
in Presence of us Witnesses

The signatures of:

Edwd: Shippen	Connodaghtoh X his mark	
Caleb Pusey	Wopechthah X	their Marks
Antho: Morris	Orettyagh X	
Joseph Kirkbride	TegoamaghsawX	
Sam¹ Darke	Shouwydagher H Harry	
	MoyonthguaghX	

On the back in William Penn's own hand:

The Indian
Kings Address
to the King
and Parliam*.

10

FIRST KNOWN LAND SALE OF THE LENNI LENAPE
OR DELAWARE INDIANS TO WILLIAM PENN, APRIL
12, 1682 (OLD STYLE).

*Now first published, from the contemporary copy, along with
the letter of William Markham, dated Upland, August 9, 1682
(Old Style). The manuscript is in a Philadelphia private collection
of the Penn Proprietary Papers, in possession of direct descend-
ants of a notable Penn Proprietary Agent.*

*Captain William Markham, Deputy Governor of the Province
of Pennsylvania, who represented Proprietor William Penn in
the Purchase, was at New Castle, present Delaware, at the com-
pletion of the transaction, at the end of June 1682.*

*In the accounts against the Penn Family the Estate of
William Penn is entered as Dr to the Estate of Lawrence Cox
(Captain Lasse Cox), deceased, as follows:*

> *"To Maintaining y⁰ Indians in
> Meat & Drink when Gov͏ͬ. Markham
> & others that came with him to
> make first Purchase of Land.*   £5.16—."

—*Penn MSS., Vol. I. 4. Accounts (Large folio), H.S.P.*

"The prices agreed upon for a parcel of Land bought of y⁰
Indian Sakamakers y⁰ 12th of April 1682 and payed them in
y⁰ end of June sd yeare

Wampam 350 fathams ½ white & ½ black

White Blanketts	20
Strawed waters fathams	20
Duffields fathams	60
kettles 4 Large in all	20
Guns	20
Coates	20
Shirts	40
Stockings paire	40

Hones	40
Axis	40
Powder 2 barrells	2
Barrs of Lead	200
knyves	200
Small glasses	200
Shoves 12 paire	12
Copper boxes	20
Tobacco Tonges	40
Small barrells of pypes	2
Sissers paire	40
Combes	40
Red Lead pounds	24
Aules	100
fish-hookes handfulls	2
Needls handfulls	2
Shott pounds	40
Bundles of beads	10
Small Saues	10
Drawing knyves	12
Anchors of Tobacco	4
Anchors of Rum 2:	2
Anchors of Syder	2
Anchors of Beere	2

Guilders .300 paid in goods:

Noat: Given in earnest to 2 Sakamakers Peuter par-ringers................2

Given To . 2. men for their Consent to remove their plantañs yᵉ Sᵈ 300 gũildˢ

Endorsed in the same hand:

Prices of a Tract of
Land bought of yᵉ Indians
April 12ᵗʰ : & paid end of June
1682: A Coppie whereof
Sent to Mʳ fforde:
Augt 9ᵗʰ: 1682

Upland Augt. 9th: 82

For frd: Philip fford:[1]

Yors of 10th mth & 20th feb: have receved ye first by ye hester & hannah y^t arryved here yesterday: I have desired ye M^r to give you an acot of his voyage. The other by ye Amity Rich^d dymond M^r yt arryved here 3d instant, the goods I have not yet on shoare from either, & am necessitated to go up this day to the falls but Leave Ralph Smith to receive what they send on shoare, I shall be soone downe again to take an accot of y^n, & by yt time hope to have more tyme & another opportunity to give you a fuller accot of things but am Unwilling to Loose this. I have here inclosed Sent you a List of goods payd the Indians that you may know what to send if not already sent

I write not to my Coz Penn in regarde I suppose him neere us, I heartely wish hee was safe arryved; for I have both Letters from Maryland & Lyke wyse news brought me by Wm haig that hath been there Latlie yt there is 2 Pyratts in Chessapeak by yt have attempted to take my Lo. Baltemore out of his house & Landed 40 men to Cary on their design; but my Lo: having advice of ym from Virginia where they had plundered severall houses, stood upon his guard & prevented ym, they gave out yt they intended to take yt Papist dog Baltemore (as they termed him) & Wm Penn—

By a Lre from one George foreman a Mart in New Yorke of ye 2d instant & another from Jno: West of ye 29th of July Last Secretary of ye sd place am informed yt a Pyrate of 12 guns & 30 men hath Lately taken a Sloope belonging to y^r goverment in wch Mr Arnold of N— Yorke was concerned 1000^l : my next will be as one with you perhaps as this. yr fore Remane

Yor reall f^d to serve you
Wm Markham

---

[1] William Penn's steward, resident in London.

Endorsed in a contemporary hand:

9th. Augt 1682
Copie of a Letter
to
Philip fforde with y[e]
prices of a tract of
Land bought from the
Indians

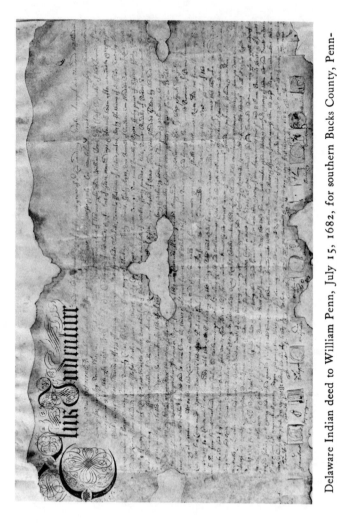

Delaware Indian deed to William Penn, July 15, 1682, for southern Bucks County, Pennsylvania. The first of the Indian grants to him in that county, it was signed at the Falls of the Delaware, now Morrisville, Pennsylvania. *Courtesy of the Historical Society of Pennsylvania*

II

DELAWARE INDIAN DEED, JULY 15, 1682 (OLD
STYLE), TO WILLIAM PENN, FOR SOUTHERN BUCKS
COUNTY, PENNSYLVANIA, THE FIRST OF THE
INDIAN GRANTS TO HIM IN THAT COUNTY. SIGNED
AT THE FALLS OF THE DELAWARE, NOW MORRIS-
VILLE.

*From the original on vellum, 20-⅛ x 11-⅛ inches, in the hand
of the non-Quaker, Thomas Revell (c. 1654-c.1709), scrivener
and court clerk, on both sides of Delaware River, in that early
day. The full transcript is as follows (H. S. P.):*

This Indenture made the ffifteenth day of July in the yeare
of o.ʳ Lord according to English Accompt one Thousand Six
Hundred Eighty & Two Betweene Idquahon, Janottowe
Idquoqu[eywon Sahoppe] for himselfe & Okonickon, Merke-
kowen, Oreckton for Nannacussey Shaurwaughon, Swan-
pisse, Nahoosey, Tomackhickon, W[estke]kitt & Tohawsiz
I[ndyan Sacham]akers of the one pte, And William Penn
Esqʳ Chiefe Proprietoʳ of the Province of Pennsylvania of the
other pte

Witnesseth That for & in Consideracon of the Sumes &
pticulers of Goods, Merchandizes, & Utensills herein after
mencõned & expressed (That is to say) Three Hundred & ffifty
ffathams of Wampam, Twenty White Blankitts, Twenty
ffathams of Strawd waters, Sixty ffathams of Duffields,
Twenty kettl[es]

ffower whereof large, Twenty Gunns, Twenty Coates, fforty
Shirts, fforty payre of Stockings, fforty Howes, fforty Axes,
Two Barrells of Powder, Two Hundred Barres of Lead, Two
Hundred Knives, Two Hundred Small Glasses, Twelve paire
of Shooes, fforty Cop[per B]oxes, fforty Tobacco Tonngs, Two
small Barrells of Pipes, fforty paire of Sissers, fforty

C[ombes] Twenty ffower pounds of Red Lead, one Hundred
Aules, Two handfulls of ffish hoo[ks, T]wo handfulls of needles,
fforty pounds of Shott, Tenne Bundles of Beades, Tenne
Small Sawes, Twelve drawing knives, ffower Anchors of
Tobacco, Two Ancho^{r}s of Rumme, [Two Ancho^{r}s o]f Syder,
Two Ancho^{r}s of Beere, and Three Hundred Gilders by the
Said William Pe[nn] his Agents or Assignes to the Said Indyan
Sachamakers for the use of the[m & their People at & before
Seal]eing & Delivery hereof in hand paid & Delivered whereof
& wh[ewith they the Said Sachama]kers doe hereby acknowl-
edge themselves fully Sat[isfyed Contented & paid The Said
Indyan] Sachamakers (ptyes to these p^{r}sents) As well for &
on the beh[alfe of themselves as] for & on ye behalfe of their
Respective Indyans or People fo[r whom] they are Concerned
Have granted Bargained Sold & Delivered And by these
p^{r}sents doe fully Clearly & absolutely grant bargaine Sell &
Deliv^r unto the Said William Penn his Heirs & Assignes forever All That or those Tract or Tracts of Land lyeing &
being in the Province of Pennsylvania aforesaid Beginning
at a certaine white Oake in the Land now in the Tenure of
John Wood & by him called ye Gray Stones over against the
ffalls of Dellaware River And Soe from thence up by the
River Side to a Corner marked Spruce Tree with the Letter
P at the ffoot of a mountaine And from the said Corner
marked Spruce Tree along by the Ledge or ffoot of the
Mountaines West-North West to a Corner white oake marked
with the Letter P standing by the Indyan Path that Leads
to an Indyan Towne called Play Wicky & neare the head of
a Creek called Towsissink And from thence westward to the
Creek called Neshammonyes Creek And along by the said
Neshammonyes Creek unto the River Dellaware alies Make-
rick Kitton And soe bounded by the Said Maine River to
the Said first mencõned white Oake in John Woods Land,
And all those Islands called or knowne by the severall name
of Matimicunck Island Sapassincks Island, & Orecktons Island

lyeing or being in the Said River Dellaware, Togeather alsoe
with all & Singuler Isles Islands Rivers Riveletts Creeks
waters Ponds Lakes Plaines Hills Mountaynes Meadowes
purtennces whatsoever to the Said Tract or Tracts of Land
Marrishes Swamps Trees Woods Mynes Mineralls & Ap-
pertennces whatsoever to the Said Tract or Tracts of Land
belonging or in any[wise] Apperteyning And yᵉ Reverson &
Reversons Remaindʳ & Remaindʳs thereof And all yᵉ Estate
Right Tytle Interest use pperty Clayme & demand whatsoever as well of them the Said Indyan Sachamakers (ptyes
to these pʳesents) as of all & every other the Indyans Concerned therein or in any pte pcell thereof To have & to
hold the said Tract & Tracts of Land Island & all & every
other the said Granted pʳmisses with their & every of their
Appurtennces unto yᵉ sayd William Penn his Heires &
Assignes forever To the onely pper use & behoofe of ye sayd
William Penn his Heires & Assignes forevermore And the
sayd Indyan Sachamakers & their Heires & Successoʳs & every
of them the Said Tract or Tracts of Land Islands & all &
every the Said granted pʳmisses with their & every of their
Appurtennces unto the Said William Penn his Heires &
Assignᵉs forever against them the Sayd Indyan Sachamakers
their Heires & Successoʳs & against all & every Indyan &
Indyans & their Heires & Successoʳs clayming or to clayme
any Right Tytle or Estate into or out of yᵉ said Granted
pʳmisses or any pte pcell thereof shall & will warrant & forever
defend by these pʳsents In witnesse whereof the said
ptyes to these pʳsent Indentures Interchangeably have sett
their hands & Seales[1] the day & yeare ffirst above written 1682

The mʳke of	The mʳke of	The mʳke of	The maʳke of
X	X	X	X
Idquayhon	Janottowe	Idquoqueywon	Sahoppe

[1] The seals are impressed on paper over wax.

The m^rke of X Merkekowen	The m^rke of Oreckton for X [hims]elfe & [Nanna]cussey	The m^rke of X Shaur[waughon]	The m^rke of X [Swanpi]sse
The m^rke X Nahoosey	The m^rke of X Tomackhickon	The m^rke of X Westkekitt	The marke of [Tohawsiz(?)]

MEMORANDA TO ACCOMPANY THE FIRST OF THE BUCKS COUNTY INDIAN LAND GRANTS TO WILLIAM PENN, AT THE FALLS OF DELAWARE, JULY 15, 1682.

A leaf, paper, in size 8 x 11⅜ inches, in the handwriting of Captain William Markham, Deputy Governor of Pennsylvania:

Memõrd

1

That they make no Differences between ye Quakers & English

2

To Take upon there Delivery of ye Land a Turfe out of The Ground To bring them (upon the Trety wth Them) to give us notice if any other Indians have any designe against us

3

Remembring our neighbouring Collonies

4

That There be a Meeting once every yeare to Reade the articles over; ye day to be apointed

5

That wee may ffreely pass Throug any of Their Lands as well y^t wch is not purchased as that wch is with out molestio[n] as They doe quietly amongst us

6

Y^t if English or Indian should at any time abuse one the other Complaint might be made to their Respective Gover, and y^t satisfaction may be made according to their Offence

7

That if at any time an English man should by mistake Seate himselfe upon Land not purchased of The Indians y^t ye Indians shall not molest them before Complant made to ye Government where they shall Receive Satisfaction.

In the handwriting of Thomas Revell:

		£	s	d
The Prizes of ye whole 600 ffathoms of wampom halfe white halfe black, white at 3 Gĩld p fathom & black at 5 Gil p fathom is..............		60..00..00		
ffalls phc [purchase?]	40 white Blanketts........	25—	0—0	
80 ^{yds}|	40 ffathom stroud waters...........	28—	0—0	
120|	60 ffathom Duffields..............	27—	0—0	
	40 Kettles 4 whereof large..........	25—00—0		
	40 Gunns.........................	30—	0—0	
	40 Kersey Coates..................	30—	0—0	
	60 Shirts.........................	15—	0—0	
	40 paire Stockings.................	04—	0—0	
X	20 mounteare Capps..............	5—	0—0	
	40 Howes.........................	4—	0—0	
	40 Axes..........................	4—	0—0	
150^l }	3 halfe Anchors powder..........	7—10—0		
	300 Small Barrs Lead..............	3—15—0		

200 Knives.......................	2—10—0
200 Small Glasses.................	3— 6—8
20 pairs Shooes..................	4— 0—0
40 Copper tŏb boxes.............	2— 0—0
40 Tobacco Tongs................	0—13—4
a small Barrell pipes.............	0—10—0
40 paire Sissers..................	0—10—0
40 Combs.......................	0—13—4
12¹ Red Lead....................	0—06—0
200 Aules......................	0—16—8
15 Pistolls......................	7—10—0
Two handfull ffish hooks...........	1— 0—0
One Handfull needles..............	1— 0—0
50¹ Duck Shott..................	1— 5—0
10 Bundles of small beades........	10—15—0
X 20 Glasse bottles.................	0—10—0
5 small Sawes....................	0—10—0
6 drawing knives.................	0—15—0
2 Anchors Tobacco..............	0—10—0
2 Anchors Rume................	2—10—0
1 Anchors Syder.................	0—10—0
2 Anchors Beare.................	0—10—0

$$240—16 \ \ 0$$
$$240—16$$

$$60— \ 0$$
$$541 . 02$$
$$4 \ \ 0$$

$$21644$$

Endorsed in the hand of Thomas Revell:

Inquire how ffarre yᵉ Indians who are here pᵣsent have p[ower(?)] to sell to begin above yᵉ ffalls.

DELAWARE INDIAN DEED TO WILLIAM PENN
FOR SOUTHERN BUCKS COUNTY, PENNSYLVANIA,
SIGNED AUGUST 1, 1682 (OLD STYLE), AT THE
HOUSE OF THE NOTED INDIAN INTERPRETER, OF
SWEDISH PARENTAGE, CAPTAIN LASSE COCK
(1646–1699), PASSYUNK, PRESENT PHILADELPHIA,
BEING A SUPPLEMENTARY GRANT ON THE BACK
OF THE DEED OF JULY 15, 1682. (SEE ABOVE.)

The full transcript is as follows, in the hand of Thomas Revell:

The Indyans Deed

Sealed & Deliv^red
in ye p^rsence of

The m^rke of
X
Kowyockhickon

The m^rke of

Attoireham

The signatures of:
   Lasse Cock
   Richd: Noble
   Tho: Revell

Memorañd That ye day & yeare withinwritten full & peaceable possession &
Seizen of the within Granted Tract &
Tracts of Land & all other ye p^rmisses
with their & every of their Appur-
teññces was had taken & delivered by
ye withinnamed Janottowe for & on the
behalfe of the withinwritten Sack-
amakers unto William Haigh Gent to
& for the withinnamed William Penn to
hold to him his Heires & Assigns forever According to ye purport true in-
tent & meaneing of ye deed withinwritten
In ye p^rsence of

   The m^rke of
     X
   Kowyockhickon

   The signatures of:
     Lasse Cock
     Silas Crispin
     Richd: Noble

In the hand of Patrick Robinson (1654–1701), the early Scotch court clerk, of Philadelphia:

First day of August 1682
Att the house of Capt Lasse Cock.

Wee whose names are hereunder written for our Selves & in name & behalfe of ye rest of the withinmentioned Sashamakers (in respect of a mistake in the first bargaine betwixt us & the withinnamed Wm Penn of ye number of Ten Guns more then are mentioned in the within deed, wch wee should have then received) doe now Acknowledge the receipt of ye sd Ten guns from ye sd Wm Penn And wheras in ye said deed there is onlie mention made of Three hundred & fifty fathom of wampam not expressing the qualitie y^r of, Wee therfore for our selves & in behafe as said is declare the same to be one halfe whyte wampam, And the other halfe black wampam; And wee kekerappamand, Pytechay and Essepamachatte Indian Saskamakers who wer the right owners of ye Land called Soepassincks & of the Island of ye Same name & who did not formerly Sign and Seal the within deed, nor were present when the Same was done, doe now by Signing and Sealling hereof Ratefie Approve and Confirm the within Named deed and the possession of the Land therein mentioned writ & given on the back thereof in all the points, clauses and articles of the Same, and doe declare our now Sealing hereof to be valeid efectuall & sufficient for the Conveyance of ye whole Lands & others within Named to ye s^d Wm Penn his heirs & asigns for evermore, as if wee had then with ye other within Named Sashamakers Signed and Seal[ed] ye Same

The Mark	The Mark	The Mark
of	of	of
X	+	X
Idquoqueywon	Swanpisse	Kekerappamand

The Mark of	The Mark of
X	X
Essepamachatte	Pytechay

Signed Sealed & delivred in pnce of us
          [*The signatures of:*]
          Nathanddell Allen   Lasse Cock

                The Mark of
                     X
                Nannechesshom

In another early hand:
Nº 2 15ʳʰ. July 1682

In the hand of William Penn's Secretary, James Logan
(1674–1751), who came over to Pennsylvania in 1699:

Lands between Delaware & Neshemineh towᵈˢ. the ffalls

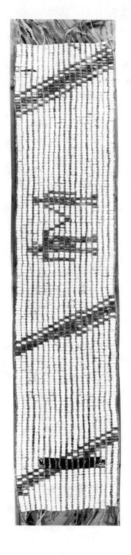

Wampum belt, 26 x 9 inches, of 18 strings. Presented to the Historical Society of Pennsylvania by Granville John Penn (1803-1867) as the gift of the Indians to his great-grandfather, William Penn. *Courtesy of the Historical Society of Pennsylvania*

12

WILLIAM PENN'S PRELIMINARY LAND SALE CONFERENCE WITH LEADING BUCKS COUNTY INDIAN CHIEFS AT PERKASIE INDIAN TOWN, PRESENT HILLTOWN TOWNSHIP, BUCKS COUNTY, PENNSYLVANIA; ABOUT 3RD MONTH (MAY) 24, 1683 (OLD STYLE).

Sassoonan or Allumpees (died 1747), later the head chief of the Lenni Lenape or Delaware Indians, stated, as reported in the handwriting[1] of James Logan (1674–1751), William Penn's Secretary, that as a boy he had witnessed the first coming of William Penn and remembered "when Wm: Penn went up to Perkasie and met the Indians there Menanget Hetkoquean and Taminy were then present."

Perkasie Indian Town, where Penn thus met leading Indian chiefs, I have determined, after long and intensive search of the original land records and assisted by a holograph letter of John Cutler, Deputy Surveyor of Bucks County, dated Middletown, 8th Month (October), 24. 1712 (Old Style), was about thirty miles north of Philadelphia, in what was later the Penn Proprietors Manor of Perkasie, and now in Hilltown Township, near present Mount Pleasant or Hilltown, and in the vicinity of the Borough of Silverdale, Bucks County. Jeremiah Langhorne was the first owner of the tract containing the Town site. Bernard Young was a later owner.

This, I take it, was the land treaty—in a preliminary way, I believe, to the land sales that soon followed—to which Penn thus alludes:[2]

---

[1] H. S. P.

[2] In a letter, dated Philadelphia, 6th Month (August) 14, 1683, to the Board of Trade, in London, now preserved in Public Record Office, London. The letter is signed by Penn himself, the main text being in the hand of a secretary, Joseph Curteis.

"I was then [about May 24, 1683] in Treaty with yᵉ Kings of yᵉ Natives for land"

He adds, "I have exactly followed yᵉ Bishop of London's councill by buying & not taking away yᵉ natives land, with whom I have settled a very Kind Correspondence."

DEED, 18½ x 13⅛ INCHES, OF THE FAMOUS DELA-
WARE INDIAN CHIEF TAMANY TO WILLIAM PENN,
4TH MONTH (JUNE) 23, 1683 (OLD STYLE), FOR THE
LANDS BETWEEN NESHAMINY CREEK, BUCKS
COUNTY AND PENNYPACK CREEK, PHILADELPHIA
COUNTY, PENNSYLVANIA, AND HIS RECEIPT,
WHICH IS IN THE HAND OF PENN HIMSELF, DATED
6TH MONTH (AUGUST) 2, 1684.[1]

There is contemporary evidence of the hospitality William
Penn extended to these Indian Chiefs, in Philadelphia, during
their sale of their lands to him. Roger Longworth (c. 1630–
1687), a well-known traveling Quaker minister of the period,
arriving from England on the ship *Endeavour*—Francis Rich-
ardson, being the Quaker master—, was staying with Penn, as
early as Saturday, 4th Month (June) 23, 1683 (Old Style), in
the Proprietor's newly built clapboard house, on Penn's own
lot, set well back from the southwest corner of Front and
Market Streets. Doubtless Longworth saw Tamany's land

---

[1] From the original, on paper, in the hand of William
Penn's amanuensis, Joseph Curteis, preserved in the Division
of Public Records, State Library, Harrisburg, Pennsylvania.
At the top of the manuscript is the modern heading in the
hand of Samuel Hazard (1784-1870), the historian, "Indian
Deed for Lands to William Penn 1683."

transfer to Penn this same day. The minister writes[1] that he stayed with Penn while in Philadelphia, and Sunday, June 24, 1683, dined with Penn along with six Indian kings. After this midday meal, accompanied by the Indians, they attended the Quaker meeting, in which Longworth preached, the Indians remaining most of the time.

The meeting was held in the Friends' Meeting House—the first in Philadelphia—built earlier in that year, 1683, of pine boards, brought from New York. It stood on a lot on the west side of Front Street, about forty feet north of present Sansom Street. Here also were held early sessions of the Pennsylvania Assembly and of the Philadelphia County Courts.

"I Tamanen this 22ᵈ. day of yᵉ 4ᵗʰ. Month Called June in yᵉ year according to yᵉ English account 1683 for me and my heirs and Assignes doe graunt and dispose of all my Lands Lying betwixt Pemmapecka and Nessaminehs Creeks and all along Nesheminehs Creeks to William Penn Proprieʳ and Governʳ of Pennsilvania &c: his heirs and Assignes for Ever for yᵉ Consideration of so much Wampum so many Guns, Shoes, Stockings Looking-glasses Blanketts and other goods as he ᵧᵉ Sᵈ William Penn Shall please to give unto me (my Parcell being much Smaller then Essepenaike's and Swanpee's) Hereby for me my heirs and Assignes renouncing all claims or demands of any Thing in or for yᵉ future from him his heirs and Assignes. In Wittnesse whereof I have hereunto Sett my hand and Seal yᵉ day and year first above written.

---

[1] Extract from the Dutch translation of Longworth's letter: "Ick was tot W. Pen ten middagsal neffens. 6 Indiaense koningen, en gegeten hebbende, giengen wij na de vergaadering, ende se giengen mede, tot de welcke 't woort des heeren in mijn hert opwess, en sij bleven de meeste tijt, van de vergaedering over."

Sealed and Delivered in y⁰ Pʳsence of *Signatures of:* Lasse Cock John Blunston Jos: Curteis	Indians pʳsent Richard Shockhuppo

Sealed and Delivered
in y⁰ Pʳsence of
Signatures of:
Lasse Cock
John Blunston
Jos: Curteis

Indians pʳsent
Richard
Shockhuppo

wittnesses
Signature of:
Gilbert Wheeler

In Penn's hand:
Metamequan   The marke of X Tamanen

In the hand of Penn:

2ᵈ-6ᵐᵒ-[16] 84
Received more severall Matchcoats[1], Stockings, Shirts, &
blanckets besides severall Guilders in Silver & I acknowledge
I have Sold all my land as above said

Tamenens X Mark

On the back in Penn's hand:

Tamanens
Conveyance to
y⁰ Pʳ. & Gʳ.

In another early hand:

23th June 1683
Tamanen grants his Lands between
Pemmapecka & Neshamineh Creeks & all
along Neshemineh Creek

In a modern hand:

No. 14   Recorded page 55 &c
           N B Boileau Secʸ"

---

[1] Made of a coarse kind of woolen cloth.

14

RECEIPT, 13½ x 9¼ INCHES, OF THE DELAWARE
INDIAN CHIEFS TAMANY AND METAMEQUAN TO
WILLIAM PENN FOR THEIR GRANT, 4TH MONTH
(JUNE) 23, 1683 (OLD STYLE), OF THE LANDS BE-
TWEEN NESHAMINY CREEK, BUCKS COUNTY, AND
PENNYPACK CREEK, PHILADELPHIA COUNTY,
PENNSYLVANIA.

*From the original, on paper (attached to the deed of same date
but not here reproduced or copied), in the hand of Penn's
amanuensis, Joseph Curteis. The full transcript is as follows:*

The 23ᵈ. of yᵉ 4ᵗʰ· Month 1683

We Tamanen and Metamequan doe hereby acknowledge
to have reced of William Penn Proprietʳ & Governʳ
of Pennsilvania &c: these following goods being the consideration for our Tract of Land Lying betwixt and about
Pemmapecka & Neshemineh Creeks and all along Neshemineh
Creek Sould & graunted unto yᵉ sᵈ. William Penn Proprietʳ &
Governʳ &c: as by a Deed Dated yᵉ 23ᵈ. of yᵉ 4ᵗʰ Month in
yᵉ year 1683 doth more plain appear being yᵉ date hereof with
wᶜʰ: we doe hereby hold oʳselves fully contented and Satisfyed.

5 pʳ Stockings:	5 hatts
20 Barrs Lead:	25 ˡᵇ Powder:
10 Tobacco Boxes:	1. Peck Pipes:
6 Coats: 2 Guns	38. ydᵉ Duffills:
8 Shirts: 2 Kettles	16 Knives:
12 Awles:	100 Needles
10. glasses:	10 Tobacco Tongs
5. Capps:	10 pʳ Sissers
15. Combs:	7 half gills:
5 Hoes:	6 Axes: 2 Blanketts
7 Gimbletts:	4 hanfull Bells:
20 fish hooks	4 yds Strode water

20 handfulls of Wampum. In wittness whereof we have hereunto sett o^r hands

The marke of MetamX-quan   The marke of X Tamanen
    ãl^s Richard

In Penn's hand on the back of the two attached documents:
    Metamequan
    & Tamanans
    Conveyance to
    me P^r. & Go^r

In the hand of James Logan:
    for ye Lands about Pemmapeck & Neshamineh

In another early hand on back:
N° 3   23th June 1683
Tamanen & Metamequan grant their
Lands between & about Pemmapecka
    Neshemineh Creeks

In a modern hand:
Recorded page 53 &c
    N. B. Boileau Sec^y

15

INDIAN DEED, 12¼ x 7½ INCHES, OF SEKETARIUS
(SECETAREUS) AND OTHER DELAWARE CHIEFS TO
WILLIAM PENN, AT PHILADELPHIA, 10TH MONTH
(DECEMBER) 19, 1683 (OLD STYLE), FOR THE LAND
BETWEEN CHRISTINA AND UPLAND (CHESTER)
CREEKS.

*Transcribed in full from the original, which is on paper, in
possession of Mrs. Francis de H. Janvier, neé Rodney, of New
Castle, Delaware, she having rescued it when torn into four pieces
from a mass of discarded papers of the estate of the late Alexan-
der B. Cooper, historian, of the same town; it is item No. 1552
in the list of over two thousand documents transferred in 1801,
by legislative act, from the State of Pennsylvania to the State of
Delaware. The main text is in the hand of William Penn's
Saxson secretary, Philip Theodore Lehnmann. The three white
witnesses inscribe their own signatures. Transcript:*

Philadelphia, yᵉ 19ᵗʰ 10ᵗʰ mᵒ. 1683

I Seketarius & Kalehickop Nochcotamen & Toonis &
Leleghanan & Wippais do hereby promise & Engage to give
or Sell all our Land lying between Christina & Upland Creek
unto William Penn Proprietary & Governʳ of yᵉ Province of
Pennsilvania, after yᵉ same manner as Keklappan & others
sell theirs in yᵉ Spring next.

Of wᶜʰ I have already received a very good Gun, some
Powder & Lead, two pair of Stockins, one Match Coat &
Tenn bitts Spanish Money.—

in wittness whereof I have sett hereunto my hand & Seal

Seketarius his Mark.
          X

Sign'd seald & deliverd
In y⁰ p^rsence of
Tho: Holme
John:Moone
John Songhurst

> *On the back of the document in the hand of William Penn:*
>> Secetarius &
>> Kalcup o^r
>> Kailops deed
>> about Christeen
> *In another contemporary hand*
>> 19th. Decemb^r. 1683
>> Lands between Christina &
>> Upland Creeks.—
> *In other later hands:*

N⁰ 15.
> [No.] 1552
> Not to be recorded

INDEX